Dancing Mockingbird

Dancing Mockingbird

Poems by

Steven Dale Davison

Cover design by Shay Culligan

ISBN: 978-1-63980-081-0

Kelsay Books
502 South 1040 East, A-119
American Fork, Utah 84003
Kelsaybooks.com

for Christine

my wife,
whose deep regard for my poetry
means all the world to me

Acknowledgments

Gravitas: "Animal Words," "Rainbow Raiment Muse"

Gyroscope Review: "Footprints"

Inscape: "The Perseids"

River and South: "Trail Maker"

Sixfold: "A Sleepless Sense of Found," "You Are Leaving"

TallGrass Writers Guild: "Desperate Squeaks"

Tatterhood Review: "Darkmoon Time"

"The Heavens on Earth," "Demon Hammer," "Carbon Units in the Petrified Forest," and "Father of Waters" are excerpted and revised from *The Road to Continental Heart: Befriending, and Defending, the Spirit of North America* by Steven Dale Davison. *Continental Heart* will be published in early 2022.

Table of Elements

Prologos

The Rail of Silence

Interlogos

A Vast Nest

Interlogos

Extra Terra

Interlogos

Elementals

Interlogos

Speak the Lake

Epilogos

Prologos

The Mind Reach Heart-deep

Before the words, the muse,
the mind reach heart-deep:
truth and beauty,
through an opened door
unto a new identity,
you spoke.
                As by gravity
I then fell through the flaming sword
into a reveal gravid paradise
of mystery knowing fruit.
Sated, I sluiced out
into the written word.
Grateful and immused,
mutable as sand and
only partially formed,
I lay naked to your spirit's
founding fire. In you I awoke
to the lively word- and line-dance,
to rhythm, rhyme, and sounds
in correspondences, to the spell of stanzas,
to the muse-ic music of poetry's promises.

I have heard your call

    at the rail of silence,
    where mountains meet the sky
    across transcendental distances;

    to the vast nest of Mother Earth
    holding creatures who, like me,
    all yearn for her arms' embrace;

with the extra terra visitation,
the cosmic and sidereal,
signs and wonders almost biblical;

as all things elemental—
the history of sand, the mystery,
the majesty, the faithfulness of trees;

in the songs the lakes and rivers make,
how they speak and scream
to me for a regard human voice;

and through it all, in the midst
of all these gifts, I feel the pull
of her daughters, the seed and sprout,
the bud and flower, the fruit and fall
of human love, the ever-muse.

Come, please, hold my hand;
make gorgeous glass of my sand.

The Rail of Silence

Mohonk Mount Escarpments

I stand in the palm of elemental handiwork
presenting sedimental sea-floor to the sky,
counting winters in ice-wedged boulders
big as rooms and old as Gaia's bones
cast free to the jumbled valley floor,
or by moments of scree rattling loose in spring.

The view here seizes the lungs, staggers the tongue.
One learns.to breathe among the beech and black oak,
to hold still when out on the open jutting slabs
of allaround and sheer down invoke inhabit
eagle screams, who claim the wind's own wings
with pinions splayed.

Light and distance, height and juxtapose
of majesty and intimacy, the plush of russet,
rose, and gold under blue, the off-white rock
enfolding lakes in the sun's radiant regard,
the flight of the ten-furlong footstool plateau,
all these transcend the ruling sense's
measure of the place.

Thought here stops at the rail of silence,
where vision, wind, and palisades
kneel forward face to face
with presence.

The Mist has Densed

The mist has densed
to a haze that grays
the sky's blue to pewter.
The ridge can't loom in this light;
it seems weirdly distant,
like a widow at a wake
sitting so still, not there,
her lovely green eyes opaque,
gazing into loneliness, unaware
of any thing but gloom
and the flensing, oncoming night.

Rainbow Raiment Muse

The road falls fast to the valley floor
    from the headwall down the ridge,
    tangent to the hamlet cradled on the flat.
The light, thin with Colorado height and rose flush,
    pales so slowly to Rocky dusk
    its patient hand feels exorable.
A little squall drifts above the quiet village streets below
    and I can trace the running line of rain there.
To see it whole and distant small like this,
    racing the slanting light—
        I would freeze this instance view.

But the four wheels are peeling down the tarmac,
    and soon we're coming level with the cloud's crown.
From here the grey mass seems parked in shafts of gold
    and my moving reference frames the storm to human scale
    till I'm a pip beside its bulk.
Then melting in and upside-down amount the top-lit hulk
    a rainbow glows. All fleet passage stops,
    and I know only moment.

But we race by and I must imagine
that the storm itself walks on
    into the cool loom and moving darkness;
that no even town could turn it;
that soon it would sag off the mountain, spent,
    while just this noon it was windflaw tumid wet,
        and yet . . .

Long past the mountain's hidden feet of night
    and all the days that since have passed,
    the moment lasts:
        the slanted shafts,
        the little ball of storm,
        the evanescent hues of the mystic smile—
    all this while, they wear for me
        the rainbow raiment muse.

Mountain Mist

A crow emerges from the mist
like a light sleeper from a dream,
closes on the spindly, half-naked elm
below me, leisurely.

A blackbird rockets away,
plunges into the soft
at mist's edge, five, seven silent
seconds across the valley.

A blue jay careens from limb to limb
in an oak, blips out inside.
The white has slunk closer now
down the wooded ridge.

The standing people do not move.
The wingèds settle in.
The night hides behind my back,
slowly foreclosing on the light.

Wild River, Fire Mountain, and Wind

Wind river swoop up slope
of fire-mountain head
    uplifting;
throw sparks and ash into clouds
    dark drifting.

Sun bright the plumes enflame above;
below, shadows reave the light,
    roving
over the shuddering mountain face
    tremor cloven.

Wild river leap off faces,
fly as mountain falls
    cataract;
splash on cooling rhyolite
    uncrystal black.

Interlogos

Trail Maker

The trail maker—
I want to meet her.

She swings me 'round the boles
of the bigger beeches,
then along a slope
with skinny naked trunks
and thin winter sunlight
through the open understory
slanting just so,
in late afternoon.

I love the little curve she made
that skirts the stone and fern there
at the bottom of the bank.

She took me through a meadow
thick with thistle and sumac
and the smell of goldenrod,
then up into the rock formations,
entered from the finest angles
for surprises in the mazes.

I want to warn her:
that orange trail
is rank with savage rose;
one year, maybe two, before
it's strangled by the thorns.
But I suppose she knows.
She goes where the tanagers nest.

A Sleepless Sense of Found

Fog gathers all night on the oak above us,
    in the meadow all around us.
As the stars step back behind the mist,
    the curled brown wetted leaves
    stitter down through the branches of the tree.
We lie close together in our bags, talking.
We steep there, we sink deeper into the share
    as points of correspondence pile up
    in layers from our stories.
My hungry tongue and lips turn demure,
    my wonder rises with the hidden moon
    until a sleepless sense of found enfolds me.

A Vast Nest

Heron

Great blue heron
    stand stately in the flow
        of even swifter tows.

Footprints

Across the meadow
    white shadows of footprints
        filled by windblow.

Helyar Wood

I went to Helyar Wood today.
The place was busy. All the furry
diggers in the duff were hurrying
and scurrying, burying their way
into winter, their little holes,
their tiny feet making sure
they have enough to eat.

A Vast Nest

Juncos peep their little secrets in the thickets.
    A blue jay scolds the frozen cover on the food.
Trees creak as the wind bends them under the weight of ice
    and rattles invisible particles against the bare bark.
Distant cracks mete out the pale of sunlight.
Around all the gloaming sounds of the wood enfolds
    a vast nest of silence.

Dancing Mockingbird

For prominence, he perches atop
a tree down by the fence.
In the back rows of his theater,
I linger, rapt, stopped by
his clarion silver tone.
His ears hear the hearts of others,
his tongue is a brother's gift,
yet he knows his own voice.
He dances as he sings:
with comic hop and flutter of wings
he punctuates his offerings with body-joy.
He speaks for a she who's otherwise silent.
Secretly, inwardly, she's smiling in her nest,
or so I do imagine.
Now I, faltering and coy,
set to with ink and pen
to emulate his ear and tongue and leap,
an altar to my muse to keep.

Snow Deer

In the thick and slowly falling snow
the apple trees loomed ghostly in the white.
They had been just about to bud.
We pushed upslope in the pearly light.

Suddenly, a windless stillness fell,
and, almost close enough to touch,
a herd of white-tailed deer appeared.
They stood with ears cocked forward,
alert, present, nonplussed. In the well
of their regard we drank our fill.

A gust then passed the moment into movement.
At ease and in/visible agreement,
they stately walked into my thankful memory.

Early Geese in the Moon of Deep Snow

What is it with the geese this season?
Is winter's end so soon?
Is winter's son so close to term
that the wingèds now are come
with the news already,
with the snow still deep
and the light still thin?

Twice now I've seen them:
four sleeps back (there were seven)
wandering roughly south;
two sleeps back four winged north
with steady purpose.
And tonight I heard them
right over the rooftops,
flying hard through the moon
by the stars.

Desperate Squeaks

A peeper the stillness peppers
with his desperate little squeaks,
saying, Here am I—find me, find me!
Alone in the dark, like the rest of us.

But he's persistent, driven by something
deeper than the silence, the absence
of an answer. Or maybe the females
of his kind don't voice their interest,

their quiet progress toward his call.
Could be he's not alone at all.
Nor am I. For now that I
truly listen, he's got my ear.
Companionship is just that near.

The Day the Bear Came into Town

In early June, the Moon of New Strawberries,
the black bear came into town.

    Young, strong, big, hungry black bear
    seeks young female in heat.

Northern home-range reigned by old boars
and eight-season she's with turf
jaws-and-claws'd up tight—
no place to make your fortune.
Hormones drive you out with her cuffs
still wet behind your ears
and somewhere . . .

Her pheromones leave her scent-glands,
float down winds, turn the nose
of heat-seeking, massive bear-boy here!

But then she was gone, who knows where.
So off he took, down the miles-long river bed,
up the little creek tangled with brush and trash,
till he found the graveyard on the edge of town.
The grass was short on roots, but he kept on digging
till the expert came with his tranquilizer gun.

A small crowd gathers, he rears to see.
A local dog catcher stands with the cops,
thrilled and fearful of a charge: he knows
a full-grown man could die if one paw fell hard
and even bullets in the heart don't stop them for sure.
The sound of nearing humans grows.
The bear sniffs indifferently of fear
and then not-mate clarity shambles him away.
The gunshot. Pott! Thckk! RRRR and rear again and
char-stum-falling slow, so slowly into the dark.

31

An oriole calls. Sssss, the move of garter snake.
Tallstick chicory in the nostrils; sunlight light.
A bass slips surface in the pool nearby.
The river guides his senses back. Muscles stack
tiers of rolling weight to paws and lift,
crack the bone-joints stiff with drugs
and truck-ride cage, shift the great weight
again and take a stride, vision bleared
but clearing, nostrils flared to gland-scent
blaring near and sweet and so heat-thick
    it makes him hard.
He stretches and scratches, bumps into the trees,
a comic sway still sloughing his gait
as he follows the pointer between his knees.

Freeze

Every limb is limned in silver;
    all is gleaming nacre underneath.
Grey the frozen pools, the depth
    between the staggered columns of the trunks.
Blue light canopies the tans of leaves,
    the darker browns of leaning boles.
A vivid wingèd, alizarin-crested,
    hangs twisted in the stillness,
    feet sunk in a branch's argent sheath.

Evening Graze

The rabbits are out for evening graze.
I disturb them but they do not run.
I sing my new song and they poise to hear.
Soon two more join and two start to play
while the others turn to the grasses, but one,
who stays to listen with twitching ears.
But she refuses my spell to come near.

Fare-Thee-Wells

Heavy fog hunkers in the hollows,
hides the high-flying honkers overhead—
a thick gray morning in the Moon of Bare Branches.

I shout out and rush to climb the steep slope.
By the time I clear the cloak of white
and mount the crown, the wedges wobble in the distance.

The air is clear and still. The hill is bare,
with spikey stubble that crunches underfoot,
a counterpoint percussion to their fading autumn-knells.

But for their raucous brag and banter
I'd have been alone in fog
and missed my chance at fare-thee-wells.

Earth Spins

Earth spins her outsweep tilt to winter
on v's of geese. The eyelids of maples
flutter on the edge of sleep. All along
the eastern rim of Turtle Island's shell,
mockingbirds sing again their farewells
to robins, voice their clarion heraldry
for those who stay.

Interlogos

Animal Words

Thick fog denses a pirouette in freeze-time.
Sound and distance founder, lost in mist and soft, dark air.
The far line of the white ice is lost in the murk-mime,
the sand sill looms silver on the frozen lap of the lake, there.
I hear your voice from farther up the carriage line,
too soft to catch the words. A horse coughs in answer.
When I find you, the mare swings her face toward mine
and you turn, your hand upon her flank, ever the dancer.
I brace to your breaths upon my cheek. You speak
animal words that make me laugh and give me thrills.
I am rendered roan and randy, stallion sleek,
and shivering in my withers, atremble at the thills.
You lean in close to scent my must and smile,
then stamp your foot and whinny, all tease and beguile.

You Mountains and Deep Water

I lie quiet, your heat seeping into me.
Alive to my body as the sky over water,
    certain moments lay,
as soothing as mist settling, as quiet as light.
In sleep as deep as shadows of mountains
    are my dreams of you.
After sinking moon drinks of lake and sun rises
I awake to the blue and deep-water eyes of you.

Extra Terra

Invocation of the Sun

A Round

Pray for the sunrise
after the sun dies;
    longest darkness
over the Earth lies.

Slowly the wheel turns;
deeply the Earth yearns
    for the fire that
down the year burns.

Night Glide

Night does not fall—it glides
in incremental frequencies
across the turning earth.
One by one the bands wink out
from pink to indigoes black.
Now the stars reach down,
tuck the once-blue blanket
under the hemisphere's chin,
and smile at the politics of refraction,
which kicks the reds out first.

Heimdall Standing on the Stair

A storm slides down the mountain to the water,
whips the waves, then moves on,
unveiling a westering sun.
On the overside of the clouds there blazes
a gold the hue of incandescent daisies;
roses, peaches, and lavender glow
on the lower beaches of their slow
and stately riverine passage.
Then, the preternatural message:
Heimdall stands atop the stair
that rises to the firmament.
Gazing down its spectral radiance
in the rainbow living air,
he declares the peace of evening.

Crescent Moon and Evenstar

Crescent Moon and Evenstar
went dancing of a sunset.
They met in azure. By indigo,
soar in love were they.
But Moon got carried away—
    oh, Milky!
Poor Star was left to set alone.
But the Winds kept singing
and the Clouds kept drifting
across the firmament's floor.
They all knew the romancing two
would meet each other again;
they'd seen the dance before.

The Perseids

In the mountain pond the stars
step out onto obsidian,
water smooth, a dark as deep
as star beams are lean.

The dome above revolves,
the last indigo fading
into background black
for the wheeling constellations.

As lightquiet counterpoint
to bullfrog songs, the moon
rises. A loon cries. The restless
winds lay down their sighs.

Through the night we doze,
awaken, snug deeper in our bag,
watch while the soundless Perseids streak
in extra terra visitation.

Earth Shadow, Swallow Moon

Earth shadow, swallow Moon? What's it mean
in my city festooned for Yuletide?
I'd know this slow advance of orbits, bodies,
geometries, as a dance, but for schooling. I'd
much sooner this lunar eclipse was mysterious.
This umbra sacra lucis—see how numinous,
how uncanny she is! Such utter disappearance
of the gleaming face of night deserves my reverence:
for see what inexorable grace redeems the light!

Humpback Moon and Trolls

Old Gibbous, the humpback moon,
hunches through the night.
She never stops, but moving stoops
to draw her lean, cold light
from the Sea of Vapors.
Her pail tips and bails out
a dimness meant for shadows.
The moon-loads of brood-light
drift down the bared backs
of two trolls who lean into the steep slope
of an open mountain meadow.
They strive to make the grade,
but their aged trunks and stupid feet
are rooted. Their limbs grope
as two trees are aspen
quaking in the wind-meet.

The Heavens on Earth

Stars. One ur-light atomized,
a billion billion balls of fire
dance across the universal hall
of vasty vaulting beams. Time rides
long on a slender bridge of light.

Nine hundred years ago
they watched the skies, astounded—
there: across the lower cusp
of new crescent moon a blaze of fire
a hundred times the size of any
other star. The observatory hums
with agitation, speculation
turns to sudden silence. For hours
the people gather. Last night
held just a simple sky.

July 4, 1054 CE.
A supernova flares. At the height
of their culture, the Anasazi flood
the sacred sites, where lines of sight
for harbinger solstice sunrise
are meted out against the canyon lands:
rock chimneys, ancient stairways,
windows in a kiva where the grid
of stone gives frame to the newborn sun
but three days a year. They had watched
and built, drawing the sacred wheel
of ceremony with their monuments.
Now this.
            Their petroglyphs
record the night: the crescent
and the mighty star are carved
on rocks all over Anasazi land.

Women must have hushed the very young
running free this special evening.
Youths, poised at adulthood's door,
stand agape, aware that this story
goes out through their grandchildren
yet to come, to the evertime—
and they are here to see it. Old folks
pray, prepare for disaster, seek
the kachinas' blessed footprints,
according to their temperaments.
Three hundred years will pass down
to their decline. By thirteen hundred,
overnight, they are gone. Why?
The twenty-three-year drought,
the change in rain, an epidemic,
Dine invaders, factions among
the people, no more wood—
no one knows . . .
                    but the stars.

Demon Hammer

Nearly changeless is the sky
from our over-vaunted human vantage . . .
till the demon-heaven hammer falls:

Ten times the light of day, at midnight,
the firestorm consumes the dark.
One hundred miles of eardrums burst
and bleed beneath the sonic blow.
The very air explodes, the four
directions disappear, the Verde River
boils away in seconds, all the earth
awakes and screams, heard all the way
to the stars. At the moment of impact
the meteorite is irresistible,
the earth unmovable.
For one split second,
the desert floor is crushed.
Kinetic force of titanic mass afire,
the nickel-iron visitation stops abruptly.
Molecules fly apart,
quantum forces rupture
the fabric of the world.
Heat, light, radiation,
all that mass converts
to conflagration and starts the fires.
Rock springs back like sponge,
debris falls for days.
The Barringer Crater cools.
Nothing living grows there—ever.
All that's left is dust of iron meteoric.

Ecliptic Apocalypse

The vast marching darkness of earth
swallows whole the moon in full,
disgorges storm, a daylong violence
of winds and tides as signs.
Oaks crash. Dunes drown,
the shoreline reaches inland,
flooding the decade's inner courts.
Volcanoes belch. The planet's mantle
quakes and splits. Cities meet their makers.
An apocalyptic century heaves
its pestilential girth up to the breach
and leers in at naked future.
From sea to darkling sea, a sinking
pyre of human hubris, throes of—

Oh, God! This horrid,
black orchid excess reeks.
A lunar eclipse, a storm,
my imagination fabricating
omens for lurid poems,
that's all. All's well.
Here, in the real world, surely,
our little fires protect us
from the business side of hell.

Darkmoon Time

In darkmoon time
the shadows eat shadows
and every thing
is thin and wailing.

Interlogos

Do Moths Not Know?

Do moths not know?

I've heard flames
look like the moon to them,
calling to their benighted brains
with silent siren light—
at a distance her face shines
with a lover's pale promises,
but the tongues of fire, they deliver
a nemesis in immanence,
an ecstasis plunge into
a seductive and razing bright.

I put all the warning words behind me.
I rode my willing wings of hope
till I was face to face with blaze,
your waxing smile fatale. So I
sped my pace and heart-long flew
into your beck and goad beguile—
and then my wings exploded.

Up their sizzling cinders drift now
on the current of a torch song,
throwing a shroud of cloud across the moon.

Mojo Clover

I'm lid-thick since your four-leaf clover,
as though—. And so
I am still in love with you.
I see the dangers and the fate,
the petals dropping onto ash,
even as I drive the long distances.
I will step into the room with my jacket open,
set my suitcase slowly on the floor.
Our seeking eyes will reach.
I will rush to lift you at the waist,
because I am strong
and you are made of scent,
and a hard kiss will not wait.
We will cut it short for the others,
who are wondering.
But a second kiss will ravage drag us
to another room and throw us on the couch
and plunge tongue deep into
our cast-off-naked press
of seeming ancient hunger now.
The couch is blazing sinking cooling slake
of questions crawling back and asking,
now what? A third kiss
will ribs engulf in arms and hands
a little chill through your dress
upon your arching back,
your golden hair my face all over,
full of nostril flare and sigh,
and not all because of that four-leaf clover—
a purpose void of why.

Elementals

First Thunder

First thunder,
    end of winter,
    robin days ahead.
All knowing
    Sun's bestowing
    new life on the dead.

Sand

1

sand   holds the laws of its movement
in the hands of others

    sea   draws and banks it
    wind   lays it up in ripples
    time   gives it dunes

        where leisurely geometries
        pace from crest to crest

2

sand   is old with its histories

    of straining and cracking,
    of water-lubed grinding,
    of moving down from the heights
    to the sea with rivers,
    of moving finer toward dust
    across an epochal passage

        stepping down from solidity,
        a particular softness obtains

3

sand   rarely finds a lasting home

    it streams into a clay pot, stops,
    and keeps shape till the pot cracks,

    or shapes into castles by hand,
    then yields to the grasp of tides,

    but: heats to a melt hot, drops
    temp, and to fuse cools glass

        without yearning, yet ready,
        embracing the guest name change

Para-Elementals

When water meets wind, mist.
When airs find earth, dust.
When fire homes in stone, magma.
Quagmire seeps the liquid earth.
Steams the boil of fire-water.
Breathing burning curls in smoke.

Kobold Cobalt Blue

Named after kobolds,
the Teuton goblins who lurk inside
the useless, ugly lumps the miners
dump on the spreading tailings heap.
They dream of riding the arsenic fumes
out from the ore in the smelter's heat
into the master monsters' lungs
and eighteenth-century history books:
cobalt—the first new metal to be refined
since the Vandals sacked old Tiber-crouched Rome.
Now they crawl from the jungles of Congo
into a new artistic confinement,
reborn as pigment in a painter's tube
or the blister of a blower's glass,
redeemed at last as the most glorious of blues.

Carbon Units in the Petrified Forest

The horned toad pokes through the rubble
hunting for insects between the jumbled
stumps of opalescent stone. She's not
a toad at all, but a reptile with a tail.
Does her DNA remember the hiss of an ancient
cousin, the crocodile-like Phytosaur,
who sunned on these very logs two hundred
million years ago before the hurricane came
for the burial? : Trees tear free of sliding banks
and crash, splash among the cycads and ferns,
sink into the ooze, lose their needles, roll
over in the surge of an upstream flood,
submerge beneath the new-laid beds of mud.
Frightened, the Phytosaur rushes out
into the rainpelt, heedless of the giant
flattened salamanders fleeing the torrent,
too, the Labyrinthodonts, who join them.
But the tree is soon forgotten.

                        Not rotten,
but lost to all organic processes
deep beneath the swampy bottom
where the mystery of inorganic chemistry
moves in: one by one the molecules
of cellulose are slow replaced by minerals,
by opals and chalcedonies, until the tree
is turned to stone. Some are crystals:
apple-green chrysoprase, bloodstone
green with drops of scarlet, redred
carnelian, orange-red sard; agate,
onyx, sardonyx layered one upon the other.
Opals have no crystal lattice, like eggs
made of jelly hardened into stone.

There they lay. Veins of brilliant color
hidden from the world while the swamp
dried up, the Phytosaur died out,
the land sank down and rose again
to face the countless seasons' rains
and winds, erosion digging to their site—
for mother Earth is ceaseless in creation.

The door of Time is off its hinges here.
Like motes of dust afloat in a geo-mausoleum,
the strew of trees: they reveal themselves
as stone turned bone of Earth most vividly,
rolled into these jumbles in the hollows,
as if, on break, some giants had left
the work lot of a sawmill ages ago,
and never came back.

To Commune with Trees

To commune with trees
I do not need my knees
or tongues tied to litanies.
I need no vocal cords
or voice of spoken words,
but only ears scored
to photo-symphonies.

Standing People Dance

sun sink west trailing cloud
line of dim advance rolling cool
lean and creak aged oak
twist and whip slender poplar
standing people dance to coming storm

Tree of Hearts

In the deep, the roots.
To the sun, the shoots.
In our lives, the branches
of chances and choices;
in good time, the fruits.
In our sentient hearing
of each other's voices,
in our caring and bearing
of each other's dooms,
in our sharing the fearing
in the face of the gloom,
    a grace blazing blooms.

Give and Rise

Between the boles the duff gives under foot.
The small clean holes that snakes make
    perforate the trail.

Quiet is the way among the grey trunks of beeches,
though somewhere near a piping bird calls.
    The green twilight pales.

Hide, you frail tiny bird in the lush bush.
Glide, you garter snake, sate of insect.
    Rise, o earth, and inhale
        the scent of the gloaming dale.

Whole for More than Just a Moment

A Healing Poem for Jason after Brain Injury

Knit bones, as even giant stones will fit
in bedrock hollows nestled under rolling plains
of dark abundant soil.

Heal brain, as rain follows peals of nearing thunder
after jagged flashes, echoing down the clefts
of deep resplendent vales.

Clear mind, as swooping thoughts like swallows dart
across the placid waters, those daughters of cleansing rainfall,
fleet and yet at peace.

All this tissue, all these cells, all are one
with wings and mountainsides, with rings of trees
and pollen on the legs of bees.

All the billion billion single lives do turn this hallowed wheel
as rivers mind the seas; and even flames of fire
are circles to the wood.

All this filling, spilling cup of yearning, reeling life
of diverse kinds frees itself from will and must
and question marks of good

by turning, pouring, homing, lusting for
the open sensate arms of mother Earth, once and always
whole for more than just a moment.

Interlogos

You Are Leaving

This monstrous looming,
distant but oncoming,
like the smoke of a burning
village cloaking the landscape,
promises a razing.
                    Ash falls,
thickening in the non-light
in a courtyard deserted of footfalls.
The fountain is dry.
                    Night draws nigh.
The scent of ends chokes out "Soon, too."

Love's Lost Demesne

The citadel has fallen.
The touch and smell and taste of you
have breached my memory's walls,
where, blind, the keening soul laments
the sharpened sense of over—and then
the edge of darkness calls,
where emptiness breeds emptiness,
where Avalon has sunk her boats
and owls hunt the rim beyond
the knowing, name, or choice
of a lover's receding voice.
Aloneness is the spiritsap of pain,
sleeplessness the landscape
of love's lost demesne.

Speak the Lake

I Sing of You Cayuga Lake

I sing a song of you Cayuga Lake,
where mist rises slowly from surfaces of dusk
and gathers light away from stars;
where days are swoops of marsh hawk
sweeping meadow slopes in silence.

I invoke your water fingers strength of countless
seasons: wash again my hidden island heart.
Let falls spend my loins. Move your breath
its spray against my timbered, stony face.
Occlude the farther shore with fog.

Splash the higher ridges with gusts of spittered rain.
Roll the heavy pouring mass between them,
loose the lightning, pump the freshet's cataractal
surge with wind and sound; pound the heaving
waves with thunder, echoes muffled in the dense.

Where the landscape arches upward, roaring waters
ride the slopes, the groping wind bends
the leaning tree, rips free the roots,
levers up the earth, upturns naked soil,
strips leaves from limbs; passes on.

The fork-lit storm recedes. Whitecaps laugh
on the lake under new moonlight. The stream,
swollen and urgent, crashes in the distance
against the lip of plunge. Mist lingers in the air again.
The outcrop glistens. A loon cries, you.

Wallenpaupack

The lake has a placid silver sheen.
High, slanting stratus clouds,
pale cream and pink underlit,
turn charcoal and crimson
as their fingers stretch across the blue.
Sunset takes its time in the overcast,
but the bat still shows against the black.
Peepers pepper the stillness
with their echoing percussive squeaks.
A catbird chatters, then goes quiet.
An evening breeze sifts through the trees
at their crowns. The cloudlight becomes
too dim to write. I fight the urge,
lay down the pen, surrender to the peace.

Lake George Elemental

Exquisite Earth and Air and Water
in ceaseless stately dance of shape and color,
movement, sound, and withal a Presence
that at times I even have an ear
in the spiritworld to hear.

Dancing in the One

I love the way it smells musty near the shore,
the way the boat rocks in the swells,
or pounds with the slaps of the whitecaps;
the sense that life glides silently below,
schools of flat-bodied iridescent bluegills
and the solitary spear of a pike,
all teeth for the strike;
the ceaseless light
a-sparkle on the water;
all manner of winds—
courteous or flirtatious,
sailor's joy or howling for a capsize,
cool, cold, or biting;
a myriad manifestation
of earth and air,
water and sun,
all dancing in the One.

Speak the Lake

Speak the lake,
 the failing Adirondack voices
 the Midwest engine forges unto death.
Feel the heat drawn out of sunlight in the leaves,
 the fish-quick shallows softened for the strike.
Smell the countless hammers raised
 in the distant curl of poison nimbus,
 a trembling weight.
Rain the tiny silver blows,
 keen the peening acid fall
 upon the anvil water face
 in thirst upraised,
 sweet, unturnable.
Hiss the thrust of yearning life
 into the deep of everlasting,
 annealing cycles into silence.
Cry the waters empty to the long lives of stars.

Lake George: Cup of Stone, Elemental Jewel

1

Cup of stone,
glaze of pine from distance,
holds full the sup of lake at sky's edge.

2

Elemental jewel,
mountain chase of stone,
air polished living waters face, the Earth adorns.

Acid Rainfire Lamentation

Heed the closing peal of thunder
rolling down the earth.
Blind the blazing sunder.

Keen then the peening fall of burn
on the anvil water face,
forging fullness into dearth.

Gasp the thirsting mountain catchment
drinking vinegar from clouds,
the javelins of rainfire.

Breathe deep and scream to stars
the ever harder gasping breath
in mouths of leaping bass.

Father of Waters

I'd like to sing the song of Old Man River like Whitman,
catalog his virtues in that long-gait rhythm free of rhyme,
true to the slow roll of current in the night,
full of smells of channel cat and silt,
the vast extent of moving water;
deep with not just history,
not just fathoms called at sunset anchor,
or drifting rafts of fiction,
not just the eons unfold geological
of ancient seas filled and dried up, lifted up;
but also with my own leaping feet over his narrow neck
as a child in northern Minnesota at the headwaters, Lake Itasca;
how the falls above Minneapolis thrilled me,
and the caves in the banks there
where gangsters hid their booze;
how the mound-builder ancestors told their tales
in snow-melt moon, while the medicine woman
starts awake with warn of flash-flood terror soon;
or the bayous, cut-off oxbows seeping and breeding frogs;
how the great rivers of the country pay their tribute,
and ask only passage to the sea;
how he makes the sidewise gate to the West and East
(hammers of the wainwrights clatter on the Westward bank,
greenhorns gawp at the hugeness of spirit on the Eastward);
how the snag floats downstream stately for silent stove amidships,
cries of crew, shrieks of drowning passengers;
suck of almost all clouds rising over Turtle Island for rain;
the bass flop after twilight.

Oh, the Mississippi rides the wide back of stone-shell floating,
Turtle Home cleanser, thirst quencher of Earth,
    Father of Waters.
And he fathers so much, following course.
The dizzy eddies sing in harmony and round, of swooosh,
spinning water-skaters, and leaves;

and the hazy light of high summer
shimmers on the brown surface swirling;
and all those molecules have been somewhere,
they're going somewhere;
and the falls throw the river out to airs' arms
and the bayous hold him close for long, till floodchange;
and tornadoes can't compare for power;
and humans ferry and bridge him, move the channel,
fish and paddle, curse and pour out poems.

He knows more about gravity and time than we,
more about the lawful power of self,
more about the awful chaos surprise,
and new birth. He gathers without question;
he answers with herons and mist;
he orders his ecos with the fullness complexity,
the simplicity of accommodation to each small niche;
but he just keeps on rollin', heart of oblivion
to the little creature plan.

Downstream Gift

Reflections on the Delaware

White Warmmoon, Scudfleece, and Sol, the Sun Prince,
keep me company on the Delaware,
stretching down from airy distances
to move upon the water,
among their own reflections dancing.

The Prince walks all around us;
one foot dances on the surface,
making short ribbons of silver skim-flicker;
the other foot skates along the bottom in the shallows,
leaving bands of light shimmering on the rounded stones
and sand, footprints of melting gold.

Old Moondisk and the Scuds prance
on top where I can see their faces
sailing on the darker spaces where
the sun's feet do not touch,
deftly dodging to the music
of the lap-drums on the shore,
the slip-slap shish-flap
of waves against the sand.

We come to some rapids;
the waves toss up and flop.
Sol breaks through the wave-crests
and flashes free in sparks of bright.
White caps flay the moon's reflection
and the clouds break up;
they can't keep the pace.

Now the Water Gap rises
in steep-angled sedimental ridges,

hammered hard by weather-blows
and falling slowly, grandly changing
faces to meet the seasons.
Hawthorne and jack pine
and other crag-dwellers
perch in notches chewed by time
    from the cliffs.
Slides slope down in grainy fields
to the road's edge and over,
aiming for the signs that warn against them.

A face appears in a rock formation
against the field of blue. He turns his head
as we change our station till he's lost to view.
If you see him plain and catch his name,
then the place must speak its secrets—
    so he turns.

A lone stone,
all robed in white and rust,
sits enthroned on a sward's crown;
the slope rushes down
from there to the road,
a near vertical domain.
Smaller rocks are dots
against the green, perching patiently,
waiting for word from their Queen.
One day word will come,
some solemn secret task;
they all will rattle down to hill's foot
    and rest at last.

Our trip is nearly done.
The Moon is gone.
The fleecy clouds still scud,
the Sun is not so high.
The paddle dips and tips.
We pass beneath a stone-piered bridge.
Then suddenly I hear (I think)
the River-spirits passing us:
an extra-elemental sound
amidst the river's dashing
flash-patting sass of foam and frolic.
Now passed into the rapids' rushing,
the sound and Presence fade;
the quick water's hurling us,
no time now to follow fairy sounds.
But after—those wind-pattern patches
skimmering on the quiet pool after white water:
could they be those same river-maidens tarrying,
laughing at our mortal craftiness?
What other hidden lives are laughing, scolding,
waiting here for the human mind to hear them?

The shifting light, the clouds,
the moon and sun,
the massive cliffs, the rift
through which the river passes—
all a gift given freely.
Sure I am the river lives
many lives all flowing into one.

Morphic Music

Salt meadow grasses seed and spread
across the sandbars stranded by the ebb.
They root, seize the shifting sediment
and build the bar towards an island,
to be always under the sun. New tides
rip out the shoots and carry them away
with clumps of earth, lay them
on another bar when they recede.
Storm waves tear the bar apart,
suck the proto-island out to sea.
Soil leaves the lift of the river
and cuts off a narrow channel
of a stream, bridging bar to shore.
Or the currents cut a new channel
where none had been before.
Grass goes to seed, silt settles,
tide and waves extend their
hands and dancing feet—
the morphic music strikes up again.

I Wish I Had Brought Wordsworth

I wish I had brought Wordsworth along.
Nobody knew the lake country better.
No one gave such song to its peace and beauty,
offered such venerate letter to the water,
the light, the trees, the movement of branches
in a breeze, the muted song of bird at dusk,
the flit of bat against the indigo husk of day,
the play of squirrels, the unfurling
of fiddlehead fern, the burn of mist
in a hidden morning glen, the unbidden
blessing of a sighting of a hermit thrush hen.
O, but that is I. My pen. My thrill. But still—
I wish I had brought the master along.
I am just a pastor in the church that he built.

Epilogos

Muse-ic Coda

So now the song has borne its coda.
The book lies finished, open in the hand.
Do resonances echo still in mind?
Do some motifs of meaning and intent
now find a vibrate home in soul?
Does the inward ear still hear
some correspondences of sound
that seek to integrate the whole?

Cool now, yes, the spiritflame
that fused these elements
of my word world. The sand
has found its final shape.
Does from the fusèd glass
some little light escape?
Have I followed faithfully
the Musèd thread unfurled
into the heart of love's labor's labyrinth,
where we and thee now meet?
Do we lay the volume down now,
slowly closed, and reluctantly?
Do we stare off silently
into an inward place
where reader and author
can face to mediated face
commune, transcend the distances,
and, musing, enter each other's world?

About the Author

Steven Dale Davison has published poems in more than a dozen journals. His hybrid book of poetry and images *The Road to Continental Heart* will be published in 2022. His chapbook of poetry, *O My Heart,* will be published in 2022. Written in both verse and prose, several of his plays have been produced. He has written both short and long fiction and has published a number of nonfiction essays and book chapters. His nonfiction book *Fifty Years of Right Sharing* will be published in 2022. Mr. Davison worked for twenty years as a journalist and professional writer in the private sector and was awarded a writing scholarship by Earlham School of Religion. He lives in Pennington, New Jersey, with his wife Christine Lewandoski.